A Year of Good-Enough Parenting:

The Frazzled Family's Weekly Dose
Of Calm and Confidence

By
MARGIT CRANE
&
BARBARA DAB

Copyright © 2013 Good-Enough Parenting, LLC

All rights reserved, including the right to reproduce this work, without written permission from the authors, except for brief passages in connection with a review.

If you are unable to order this book from your local bookseller, you may order from Amazon.com, CreateSpace.com, or from Good-EnoughParenting.com

The techniques described and the advice given in this book represent the opinions of the authors, based on their experiences. The authors are not licensed to practice medicine and, therefore, expressly disclaim any responsibility for any liability, loss, or risk, personal or otherwise, which is incurred as a result of using any of the techniques or recommendations suggested herein. If in any doubt, or if requiring medical advice, please contact the appropriate healthcare professional.

ISBN-13: 978-1490448459
ISBN-10: 1490448454

Printed in the U.S.A.

ACKNOWLEDGMENTS

Margit would like to sprinkle love and fairy dust on her miracle-family & miracle-friends, particularly her wonder-husband Nick (her biggest fan), and her friend and business partner, Barbara "Sparkles" Dab (a brilliant light who brightens up my life and laughs at all my jokes). You rock, Sistah!

Barbara would like to thank, first and foremost, her children. Without these angels, her world would truly be an empty and boring place. To John, the love of her life, husband and best friend, well, you know... And last, but certainly not least, to Margit Awsum Crane, thank you for the ride of a lifetime!

MARGIT CRANE & BARBARA DAB

INTRODUCTION

This is not a parenting book; it will, however, make parenting easier, so that's pretty cool.

To get the most out of this book, we've divided it into 52 weeks. That way, you have 52 inspiring stories! Each of the 52 stories has a suggestion for you, something to consider during the week (Just one. No extra thinking involved. That's how we roll.)

Give yourself permission to skip some weeks, or to start in the middle. Go back or look ahead. If you're not up to doing one of the suggestions, no worries. There isn't one way to read this book – do it your way. Your way is good enough.

So throw away your doubts, dive in, and join the Good-Enough Parenting Nation. After all… **Good enough is the new perfect!**

Love & Hugs,

Margit & Barbara
July, 2013

MARGIT CRANE & BARBARA DAB

The Good-Enough Parenting Manifesto

(The complete text of the Manifesto can be found on our website, Good-EnoughParenting.com)

1. Good-enough parents can act with courage, even if they're not feeling courageous.

2. Good-enough parents don't lecture, yell, nag or act smug ... much. Good-enough parents don't withhold love.

3. Good-enough parents live in the present ('coz that's where your kids live).

4. Good-enough parents work really, really, really hard not to take things personally.

5. Good-enough parents have house rules and everyone in the family understands these expectations.

6. Good-enough parents take time for recreation, hobbies, and their own friendships.

7. Good-enough parents get guidance and support when they're struggling with a challenge.

WEEK 1
An Alternative to New Year's Resolutions

If New Year's Resolutions worked, I would be a fan. My experience, though, is that resolutions are a set-up for failure and self-criticism. Not interested. Instead of New Year's resolutions, I choose a New Year *Theme*.

1. A theme can be a **personality trait** like: friendly, forgiving, calm, OR
2. It can be an **action** you want to do more, like: exercising, eating healthy, not swearing, OR
3. It can describe a **role** you play (or want to play) in the world, like: artist, friend, son or daughter, OR
4. It can be a **quality** you want to

strengthen: non-judgment, love, prosperity, OR
5. You can take a **line or phrase** from a book, movie, or song.

Of course, they should be positive themes, *not* like "judgmental," or "couch-potato."

Then choose one for your theme of the year. Here are some of my themes from the last few years: *Year of Soaring, Year of Receiving, Year of Love*, and this year's theme: *Year of Transparency*.

How does it play out? Well, this year, my intention (transparency) is to just let myself be me, with all of my warts and scars. I'll be truthful and vulnerable.

I also like to choose a photograph or make a collage to post on my wall. I find that in a busy world, it really helps to have a picture that grabs my attention as I zoom by. I can then remind myself to refocus my attention.

With your thoughts consistently directed toward a theme, you become more confident, less stressed, and more likeable. Yup, all that.

WEEK 2
Let's Not Judge Ourselves or Others

Let's talk about those parenting books that have sarcastic titles about how dysfunctional we are as parents. Sure they offer a light-hearted, edgy approach to raising children, but there is something inherently distasteful about using profanity, violence, booze, self-criticism, or scatological jokes when referring to parenting.

It's not that I don't have a sense of humor, I just believe strongly in the power of words. I have a friend who belongs to a mother's group. They've named themselves "The Bad Mothers Club." I know it's supposed to be a joke, but my friend is fraught with insecurities about being a single mom, raising a teenage daughter. She's dealing with some heavy, real-life issues that test her everyday. And she's a great mom! She's concerned, she's involved, *she's there!*

Maybe using names like "The Bad Mothers Club," "Sh-tty Mom," "Drunk Mom," "Crazy Mom" gives a voice to our deepest fears, kind of like whistling in the dark. But is there a line that gets crossed with the constant repetition? **Do we start to believe we are bad parents, even subconsciously?**

Let's not judge each other or ourselves. Good-Enough Parents are good enough and we should be reminded of that everyday, no kidding!

WEEK 3
Do I *Have* To Do Chores?

I am no Domestic Goddess. When it comes to chores I am *just* like your child or tween that whines and complains about having to do anything that interrupts that very important TV show, computer game, or Facebook conversation.

I know this about myself. My job, now that I know this, is **to make it "okay" to do things I don't want to do**. You can do the same for yourself and/or your kids.

Here are some suggestions that work for me and my clients:

1. Don't call them "chores." Call them "Helping the Head Elf" or "Avoiding Trouble Down the Line." Something

clever or catchy.

2. Turn chores into a game, like a scavenger hunt or a treasure hunt. You can hide clues or pennies or dried fruit pieces or stickers.

3. Combine chores with exercise, either before or after. For instance, you can make an obstacle course. Like: Run around the couch and each time, pick up something from the floor and put it where it belongs. Keep the kids (or Margit) moving and you kill two birds with one stone.

4. Put on some music. Chores = drudgery. Make it fun by having a dance-off or a clean-off or just something where everyone's shaking her booty. You will amuse your kids, and laughter makes *everything* better.

Do what works for your family and, for gosh sake, have some fun!

WEEK 4
The Power of Positivity

My mother was an eternal optimist and the most positive person ever. Her favorite saying was "You can catch more bees with honey than you can with vinegar."

My dad, on the other hand, was a realist and he sought to protect his children from the more gritty details of the world.

As a parent I've tried to have a balanced outlook. I wanted to protect my kids from some harsh realities, but I also didn't want them to grow up fearful or mistrustful of the world. I wanted them to be confident in assessing risk and deciding when to try new things. And, I wanted them to believe in the basic goodness in everyone.

Here are a few things I learned along the

way:

1. *Children come into the world with their own psychic blueprint but love, stability and safety make a big difference.*

2. *When someone spills milk at the dinner table, just say "Ooooh, the milk spilled!"* BTW, this works for bigger "messes" too! A bad grade, a speeding ticket; poor decisions are all part of the deal. Teens know when they've messed up. No need to rub it in.

3. *You **really can** catch more bees with honey.* A smile, a pleasant tone, a "please" go further than barking orders or making assumptions.

4. *When all else fails, count to ten and then give a hug!* Before you yell or say something you know you'll regret, leave the room, count to ten, take a deep breath and then go give them a big hug. If they push you away, it's okay! They'll come around, I swear!

My dad used to tease my mom about being a pushover or just seeing things through rose-colored glasses. But my mom was no pushover and I'm telling you the view from these glasses is pretty sweet!

WEEK 5
Sticks and Stones

When I was a child, I was very insensitive. It's true. Everything that happened was about me and how would I be affected and what would people think and would this *thing* ruin my life?

In case you're rather new to the ADHD scene, this is not uncommon among "my people." One time, I spent an hour planning how to make one of my mom's friends feel bad about an injury she had.

I was bullied in school, by a couple of girls, but I was also a bully – noticeably pointing at and walking away from the kids that supposedly had "cooties." I still remember them clearly.

I'm not proud of this. I've always been very insecure so I can say, for sure, that my cruelty came from a daily sense of foreboding that things weren't right in my world and so I needed to have the upper hand.

A friend of my mother, though, gave me a good lesson about the effects of cruelty on another person:

She was a seamstress and so, of course she had lots of fabric. She had me choose one of the more delicate pieces, and she cut it into the shape of a heart. She talked to me about how fragile that heart was, and that just because we don't *actually* break someone's heart, name-calling hurts a lot.

She told me, "That's your heart, Margit, so you want to protect it." I nodded. "But, every time you hurt someone's feelings, you need to make a cut into this fabric heart." Gosh, did I feel horrible. After that I tried for the rest of my life to do the right thing. I wasn't always successful but, boy, did I try.

Eventually, I became a woman I could admire; the woman I am today!

WEEK 6
Parenting is a Marathon

From the moment I knew about the first tiny life I was growing, I was head-over-heels in love. And, honestly, I still am. The years have flown by, to be sure, but they've also been full. Full of sleepless nights, exhausting days, battles over homework, tears over friendships, victories large and small, abundance and loss, grief and joy. And here's the best part: it's not over, not by a long shot.

I love learning more about my children as they grow and I learn about myself in the process. The teenage years were the most confusing and challenging for all of us. Somehow we survived, though not without some wounds.

I confess, I was pretty quick to protect and defend my daughter and sometimes didn't let her fight her own battles. I eventually learned to trust her to take care of herself and encouraged her to be her own advocate. Mostly I tried to let her know she was loved and that she mattered.

These days, my daughter is figuring out the adult world and I watch her struggle to find herself in this new identity and even at her age, it's tempting to jump in with advice. But just like when she was learning to walk and suffered numerous bumps and bruises, I have to let her stumble, fall and pick herself up. And I keep letting her know that she is loved and that she is not alone.

It's a marathon, so pace yourself.

When I look at my beautiful adult daughter, I see the entirety of her life up, from precious newborn to defiant toddler to clingy middle-schooler to rebellious high-schooler, and beyond. And someday, maybe, she'll be the nervous new mother. And that will be another chapter in this adventure. It's a marathon not a sprint so *dig in and enjoy it because it's the best ride of your life.*

WEEK 7
The Grinch That Stole Valentine's Day

I don't really want to do away with Valentine's Day, but why can't it be every day (Or every other day. Or once a week)? And without the stupid candy.

Here's the deal: **What kids want, more than money or presents, is *your time*.**

In my family coaching practice, I ask kids all the time what they'd like to change in their house. All of them, even the 17-year-old girl, who calls her father, "My mother's husband," want more time with her parents. All. Of. Them. Candy is so far down the list that kids think I'm ridiculous when I suggest it.

I know all of you are working parents - either at home or outside the home. We all have super-busy lives. **But your children want to see you and they want you to see them.**

I am particularly enthusiastic about doing things together, even mundane daily chores. Instead of creating separation in your family, where everyone has a few responsibilities, and then they go off to their separate worlds, how about creating chores that are done together?

They're still learning the skills you want them to learn - cleaning, washing, drying, sweeping, folding, making meals - but they're just doing it with company! *I, myself, will do many more things if I have company.* And if they want to do it alone, and it gets done, fabulous. Whatever works.

There are lots of ways to spend time with your kids. If you need suggestions, ask them. They think about this all the time. I had an 8-year-old client who asked that the family come outside to play for just 15 minutes a day. How simple is that?

If you want to celebrate Valentine's Day, go ahead. But could you do it every day?

WEEK 8
Stressed-Out or Successful?

This week I had a very enlightening phone call with my older son. He is a concert pianist, and he shared a conversation he had with his teacher. She discussed one of her students, a 14-year-old boy who, in addition to being a promising pianist, is also a competitive swimmer. He also speaks several languages and is a star student. She described his high-achieving parents and the other siblings in the family and said to my son, *"You know, he's a real kid."* To which my son respectfully replied, *"No he's not. He's just doing what his parents are pushing him to do."*

She then asked my son to describe his parents. I held my breath waiting for his answer.

After a pause, he said he told his teacher that we had always supported him but never made him do anything he didn't want to do (well almost anything). "She probably thinks we're hippies," I joked, and asked him if he wished we had been pushier with him. He just laughed and said no, he'd had a great childhood and couldn't imagine missing out on any of those other things.

Don't get me wrong, kids need encouragement and at times some tough love in order to learn the consequences of their actions and choices. But the world is filled with so many amazing opportunities and we believed it was our job to expose our children to those we thought were important and let them find their own way. Yes we guided them, yes we were firm at times. *But their choices and accomplishments are theirs, not mine.* Am I proud? Darn tootin'!

Do I take credit for providing a climate where creativity and exploration can flourish? Absolutely! *But his accomplishments are his, not ours.* As parents we are often so focused on the future that we forget that our kids only get one childhood. And don't we want them to remember that fondly?

WEEK 9
Delayed Gratification is the New Cool

The New Cool (as I'm declaring it) is **not** getting what you want, at least not right away.

It's like dating. (Bear with me!) Most people would agree that it's not a good idea to date someone once or twice and then get married. Many people would agree that it's probably a good idea to date more than one or two people (not at the same time) before getting married.

So what if we "dated" those things we think we need? What if we wooed them, saved up money and stored up our passion for a bit? What if we took the time to see if that toy, game, shirt or phone is a "fling" or if it's really a good fit for our child, *at this time?*

Getting stuff actually isn't that satisfying in the long run. Take it from me. I got stuff. I got tons of stuff. My parents desperately wanted to be good, loving parents, but it doesn't work that way. It actually did more to drive a wedge between us because the "Stuff" became a parent-substitute. No parent wants that...

What I didn't get were many life lessons. My parents didn't teach me to share, for instance. I learned that when I was 33 years old (no kidding). I learned that it's okay to ask for help when I was 36. I learned to collaborate, to work in a team, when I was 40. *If you don't teach your kids, someone else will and it may not be what and when you want it to be.*

Waiting feeds the power into life and its lessons. Waiting teaches how to be resourceful, how to be creative, how to dream, how to collaborate, and how to set goals and plan to achieve them.

This year, be a cool parent - the New Cool. Teach your kids to wait. Teach them to make a plan. They probably won't thank you but that's only because they won't realize that it could've been worse. **And that's a great thing!**

WEEK 10
Love Affair With An Alien

Ah, love! Is there anything sweeter? When my kids were babies, I'd look at them sleeping in their cribs and my heart would melt. They were so innocent, so sweet, so beautiful.

Fast forward several years and I could swear aliens came in the night and swapped my little angels for creatures I no longer recognized. What now stood before me was some alternate reality.

Teens aren't that adorable. They morph into an awkward, uneven version of what will be their adult selves. There are hormonal swings, mood swings, breakouts and breakups. There's yelling, crying, and stomping out of the room. It's just not a pretty picture. *So how can we parents survive and even grow closer to our little teen darlings?*

I remember like it was yesterday the first time my daughter pounded up the stairs yelling "I hate you!" I won't lie, it hurt. That night after a very difficult evening routine, when she was finally asleep in her room, I quietly opened her door and went in. I stood over her sleeping 13-year-old form, listened to her even breathing, looked at her peaceful (finally) little face and felt that old familiar flood of love and wonder at my beautiful girl. All my anger and frustration from the day faded away and I just felt unconditional love and compassion for what she was going through.

During the turbulent times it always helped to repeat the ritual of silently slipping into their rooms at night to gaze at their slumbering faces, to remember the babies they once were and marvel at the adventure unfolding right before us.

WEEK 11
Warning!
Random Acts of Parenting Ahead!

Sometimes it's so tempting to be a kid again. I think about it a lot. But I'm not a child anymore and there are young ones who need me to be the adult.

I call this Parenting Synergy – it is the powerful, wonderful connection that's created when parents accept their parenting responsibilities and let the kids be kids.

Think of two magnets. When you put two positive sides together, there is no connection – the magnets repel each other. Similarly, with families, when child and parent are both trying to be kids, or when the disciplinarian parent expects the child to be adult-like and to perform superbly all the time, the two will repel each other and parent and child will disconnect. *The only way to be connected is for the parent to be the parent and the child to be the child, and that means that "Random Parenting" or parenting whenever it suits you, cannot work.*

Here is the Best Reason Ever to parent with clear, consistent and kind boundaries, both for your sanity and for your children's sanity:

Boundaries and consistency keep children safe and help them *feel* safe. For children, knowing where the limits are encourages them to courageously explore the world while feeling secure that home remains as it always has been – a safe and loving refuge from the sometimes confusing or frustrating aspects of growing up.

Boundaries and consistency teach courage, curiosity, security, love, decision-making, non-judgment, kindness and goal-setting.

So stay with it, parents! And know that being a parent is so much more than being a police officer, a maid, a chauffeur or a baby-sitter.

You are creating world leaders, all of you.

WEEK 12
A Room of Their Own

When my kids were growing up, I was very sensitive to their privacy and boundaries. If their room was messy, so what? I had control of the whole house.

Now, personally, I do not like mess and clutter. Most of my house is pretty well organized and orderly. My own bedroom is organized (except for the nightstand on my hubby's side of the bed – Love you, Honey!). But here's the deal: I don't have to live in my kids' rooms! If they enjoy living in mess and clutter, that's their business. I can simply close their door. Out of sight, out of mind, baby!

We did have rules about the mess,

though. They couldn't keep food rotting in containers, there had to be a clear path to the door or window, and they could not complain that they lost something in there.

This permissive messiness did not carry over to the rest of the house. Common areas had to be kept neat and tidy, and the kids had chores and responsibilities. But I was not going to battle over an unmade bed or clothes on the floor. My kids spent summers at camp and learned well how to take care of their surroundings and respect others' things.

When they left home for college, they knew how to live with others. And their own homes are pretty neat. Trust your kids. When the time comes to leave home, they'll know what to do.

Allowing a child to express herself is priceless, as my own experience as a teenager taught me. So, breathe, and do yourself and your kids a favor and let them have their rooms!

And be grateful that you don't have to live in there!

WEEK 13
Balancing Self-Care with Child-Care

The most burning, universal questions I hear from parents have to do with the boundaries between caring for yourself and caring for your children. Am I being selfish? vs. How do I stay sane and healthy? Tough questions, for sure.

Are you being selfish? Not necessarily, but let me ask: are you ignoring a budding (or festering) problem, hoping that it will go away on its own? In that case, I would say that it's important to pay attention. *Actually, it's coming up because it requires your attention. Things that don't need attention don't rear their ugly heads!*

Ignoring the challenge actually guarantees that it will get worse. Time well-spent now will almost always ensure that you won't need to perform "triage" later, when the problem has become bigger and multi-layered.

On to the second question - making sure that you're taking care of yourself:

Anxiety, depression, dependency on outside sources (including TV or Facebook) are signs of too much stress, and stress compromises your immune system. That's serious stuff. A compromised immune system leads to system failures, more anxiety, more depression, weakened thinking, and weakened executive functions such as time management and problem-solving – key skills to have as a parent. In fact, the problems that arise from stress will just stress you out more.

Sacrificing your life is counterproductive. I subscribe to the "Oxygen Mask Theory." Take care of your health first so that you are available to take care of your child's health.

WEEK 14
Truth or Consequences

Sometimes "telling the truth," or "keeping a secret" is just a sneaky way to refer to gossiping. "You'll never guess what I heard today!" If you have to hide it (as in gossip), it's not the best policy to live by.

The other type of secret, which is perhaps the more damaging, is the omission of details. For example if someone were sick, growing up we'd be told just enough to get the gist but not the whole story. Now this strategy is fine for younger children who might not understand the details or might be frightened. But for tweens and teens, I believe honesty is the best policy.

I've spoken to parents who say they are protecting their kids from being confused or anxious upon learning the truth about a family member's illness. But the real truth is that kids become more confused, anxious and mistrustful when they sense there's more to the story and their questions go unanswered.

Parents also rob their teens of learning valuable coping skills by keeping mum about difficult situations. Life can be messy, harsh and downright sad. But, as kids mature, it's critical that we adults teach them that they have the resources to weather the bad times. These are teachable moments.

When my kids were in their early teens, we lost both of my parents one after the other in a very short period of time. As hard as it was and as sad as I felt, I tried not to sugar coat the truth and to answer their questions as directly and honestly as I could.

Teens are smart, intuitive and sensitive, and believe me, what they will imagine in their minds will be much worse than the reality. So do yourself and your family a favor and make honesty the best policy.

WEEK 15
That's Not My Job!

Our family doesn't fit into a nice neat category, and I'm betting yours doesn't either.

For example, at different parts of our lives together, both my husband and I have taken turns being the main breadwinner. Also, my husband is the more patient, giving, clean-up-the-messes parent (and grandparent). I'm more of a mix of practicality, love bombs, and fun. He's steady; I dart in and out. My husband will do the "What do you need and how can we help?" type thing. Cooking, cleaning, bill-paying? Husband, husband, husband.

Need help with homework? That's me. Need to talk to a teacher or school principal?

That's also me. Need to talk to a police officer? I'll go with my husband but he'll do the talking and I'll do the praying (not that that's happened). Medical crisis? Well, let's just say I'm somewhat of a germaphobe!

I confess that this bothered me for a long time. I know that I'm a "Square Peg" type person and, yet, the pull to have a stereotypical family is strong in our culture.

My advice, for what it's worth: Do what works for you, no matter what it looks like to others. *The trick is making sure that no one person carries the whole weight of responsibilities and that you show respect and gratitude for the work or help that each member offers, whether "that's their job" or not.*

Thank your kids for bringing their dishes to the sink. Thank them for feeding the dog. Tell them how much you appreciate them getting through a tough moment without yelling. And teach your children to thank you for going to work, for making dinner, for taking them on a vacation.

We all want to feel that we matter to someone, square peg or not.

WEEK 16
Food for the Soul

What's the big deal about family dinner? The most important answer to that question is that *it's not about the food*. Coming together in the evening as a family allows us all to check in, share our day's activities and communicate whatever is on our minds. Heck, sometimes dinner is the only time we spend all together and even if it only lasts 30 minutes, it packs a real punch.

I recently spent time with some family members who don't "do" family dinner. Everyone wanders in and out of the kitchen at will and warms or throws together whatever they want, then sits down at the kitchen table, often alone, to eat. The behavior is the same for weekend breakfast and lunch. This family includes two pre-teens and a teenager. I tried to no avail to create some family meals. The best I could muster was a Saturday morning breakfast with two of the kids.

You can customize your version of "Family Dinner" if the concept of preparing dinner every night seems overwhelming. Keep in mind the meal doesn't have to be fancy or even prepared by Mom or Dad. Dinner can be pizza or takeout Chinese. For that matter, it doesn't even have to be dinner. Maybe in some families, everyone is around for breakfast or lunch. The idea is to create some sacred time for everyone to come together, and to commit to doing it regularly.

Of course, don't expect 100% success all the time. Shoot for 50% or 80%, or whatever works for your family. And let everyone in on your plan. No need to ambush them!

Family meals feed the soul - the years fly by and in the blink of an eye, everyone is off on his own. Family dinners create memories and allow everyone to savor the time under the same roof. Start now. Make this the week you start cooking up some food for your family's soul.

WEEK 17
Albert Einstein, Parenting Coach

Are you so busy being strong that you don't have time to ask for help? Do you come from a culture or family that values...

- self-reliance?
- pushing through a problem 'til you get to a solution?
- keeping family problems within the family?
- putting on a happy face regardless of what's happening inside you?
- hard work over emotional well-being?

If so, Albert Einstein wants to talk to you!

Noted physicist and all-around genius Albert Einstein famously said, *"No problem can be solved from the same level of consciousness that created it."*

In plain English this means: Stop trying to solve all your problems because you can't. In short, sometimes, we need help.

The trick is to know when to persevere vs. when to get support. So I've created this easy Time-to-Get-Help Guide:

1. **You're stressed.** Stress is a big neon sign that tells us that something is off, especially if you're trying to cover it all up with TV, a bit o' boozing, over-eating, yelling at the family, and so on.

2. **You wonder whether you need help.** People who are functioning well, don't ask if they're functioning well. They just do it. How many times do you ask, "Do I need help buttoning my buttons?" Kind of absurd, right? That's because you don't need help buttoning buttons.

3. **You feel there's no one who can help.** When you think no one can help you, that means you're looking for help. And you're in luck! You wouldn't believe how much help is out there until you start asking for it.

If Albert Einstein can't solve his own problems, I'd say we're in good company!

WEEK 18
Weathering a Family Storm

A couple of weeks ago, my brother was hit by a taxi as he was crossing the street. After spending a few days in the hospital, he returned home to rest and recover from a skull fracture and concussion.

While their dad was under the watchful eye of doctors and nurses, I was able to have some fun with my niece and nephews. They could relax.

But reality set in once Dad was home and on the mend. I saw first hand how each member of the family reacted to the crisis and, without judging, I made some observations that might be helpful during times of stress.

1. Try to maintain a semblance of a

"normal" routine. Whatever "normal" is for your family, make the effort to keep to it.

2. Let each child know what is happening and why, and tailor it to his age and personality.

3. Don't be afraid to ask the kids to help out, even if they normally don't. Let them know their assistance and participation is important and valuable to the family during this period of time.

4. Help your kids express their feelings. Some kids are very verbal, others are not. Perhaps the not-so-verbal ones need to draw or sing or punch a pillow. Just because someone doesn't talk about her feelings doesn't mean she doesn't have them. Don't judge the one who withdraws, just let him know you are there whenever he's ready.

5. Take time for yourself! If you're running on empty, out of control or exhausted everyone else will feel it. Do what you need to do to stay centered during this time. And look for support. Don't be afraid to appear weak or needy.

WEEK 19
Not Good Enough. Not Even Close.

Enjoy this tongue-in-cheek view of what **not** to do:

1. **Lecture, yell, nag, and be smug**.

Who doesn't love to cuddle up for a good lecture? And yelling just makes it that much easier to be heard. Of course, if you're one of those "good-enough parents" who doesn't believe in yelling, acting smug works great, too.

2. **Teach your kids to be perfect**.

Mistakes are very, very bad. Everyone knows that people who make mistakes never learn and are branded as losers for life. No one will hire them and, for sure, no one will marry them.

3. **Project negative thoughts about your child's future.**

Repeat them quietly to soothe yourself to sleep: "My child will never do anything right." "My child will end up working at a fast-food joint." Jump right in and swim around in your fears until you have no hope left at all.

4. **Withhold love.**

You've said "I love you" once; what do they expect? Especially when they're SO demanding. They're like little developing people, or something.

5. **Don't have any rules or routines.**

Rules and routines make life so predictable and calm. Rules and routines can teach time management, follow-through, respect, cooperation and interdependence. Blech.

And remember, help is for wusses. Never ask for help!

WEEK 20
It's All About the Shoes

One of my nephew's quirks is that he enjoys sharing his "wisdom" about life. He recently shared a story with me about the time he attempted to visit the school library during class without that all-important "Hall Pass". He walked into the library only to be turned away by a teacher. Undaunted, he went to his locker, changed from his sneakers to his "lucky shoes", and returned to the library. This time around, the aforementioned teacher was busy with other students, so he was able to get in, get what he needed and get out. *"You see,"* he told me, *"It's all about the shoes."*

I asked him to explain. He grunted something about feeling better about himself when he wears the shoes.

I've been thinking about this story. Here is a very intelligent, adorable, funny, talented kid who has many friends, but underneath it all is an insecure little boy trying to figure out where he fits in the world. When children are very young it's appropriate to carry a blankie, a pacifier, a doll or something else that makes them feel safe. But for older kids, that special object needs to be more incognito.

As our kids become teens, it's easy to forget that underneath all the bravado, the bad attitude and the generally unpredictable behavior, lurks that insecure little child trying to find his way in a confusing world. So when your teen seems fixated on what to you feels random or insignificant, remember: it's all about the shoes. Give your blossoming adult a hug, show some compassion and let them know they're going to be okay.

And let's face it, don't we all have that one thing that makes us feel we can take on the world? For me, it's a rockin' pair of black pumps (See? Shoes!).

WEEK 21
The Kids Are Watching

I live across the street from "The Perfects." I must admit that I don't know them at all, except to say "Hi" on occasion, but after six years of living across the street and watching their kids grow, I consider myself an authority (haha).

Here's why they're perfect:

1. Their house *never* needs a new coat of paint.
2. Their landscaping is always pristine.
3. They have two teenagers and I've *never* heard any yelling.
4. Oh, and here's the weirdest thing to me: They *all* participate in yard work once a month. Those parents must offer some pretty perfect bribes!

As parents, we teach our kids to behave the way we do, even if we don't intend to. So be the kind of adult you'd like your kids to become. Be the kind of adult you'd like your kids to *marry!*

Think about:

- How often do you complain?
- How often do you look away when people are speaking to you?
- How often do you interrupt?
- How often do you push, elbow, or punch?
- Where are your manners?
- Do you do what you're asked when you're asked, or do you put it off?
- Are you around for breakfast, dinner, special occasions?
- Do you denigrate your spouse?
- How much time do you spend with the family?
- Do you say things to be funny but they're actually hurtful?
- How often do you find ways "to escape" the family?
- How often do you blame other people?
- Are you a bully or an encourager?

We don't have to be perfect, but we can always be better. Our kids are watching.

WEEK 22
Mom, I Got This.

My youngest started preparing to head off to college a couple of years ago. After each college tour or open house I'd be all charged up but of course, he didn't like all of the same places I did. "You don't want to go there? It's so beautiful and so prestigious," I'd say. To which he'd respond, *"You know mom, my college experience is really all about you."*

The first time he said it, I confess, I was truly caught off guard and felt pretty embarrassed. But now it's become our little code, his way of saying, "Back off, Mom, I've got this."

As I look back over my two-plus decades of parenting, I really think this is at the heart of being a Good-Enough Parent: *being present, in the moment, and realizing it's not all about me.* Yeah, there's a lot to deal with. I've been exhausted most of these years, had spit-up on my nice clothes, a messy house, run late to meetings, cried on the phone to my mom, shrieked on the phone to my husband. But through it all, I also somehow had the sense that it would be over in a heartbeat, and that I'd miss it.

Raising teens is challenging on a good day. On a bad day, it can bring you to your knees. But keep the time travel in check. Stay in the moment; that's where your children live. They fear what you give them to fear – they're excited about their future. You be excited too.

Listen to your kids. Their life really is theirs, not yours.

Use it to make a connection with your child, but don't let it define your vision of him. Stay in the moment and really listen to him. This is your teen's life, not yours, and they're dying to talk to you about it but they're afraid you won't hear them.

Remember my son's secret code, "My life is really all about you." NOT!

WEEK 23
Two-Foot Teacher

Now that I'm a grandma, I am reminded that parenting can be much simpler than we make it. Here are the ten most important reminders I've gotten from my 18-month-old granddaughter.

1. Smile at your kids, nod your head when they speak, look at them, laugh at their jokes, reach out and touch them. This is how brains process appreciation and approval. (I read that somewhere.)

2. Play outside a lot. Take walks, throw a ball, shoot some baskets. We all need time outside.

3. Talk to your kids. Tell them about your day. Tell them what you love about them.

Tell them how happy you are to be their mom or dad.

4. Listen to your kids. Listen to what they have to say about their day, their friends, their mistakes, their triumphs, their opinions on large or small issues that affect the world.

5. Speak gently. No one feels closer and more connected to a person who yells at them.

6. Kids don't need a lot of fancy stuff to be entertained. The world is an interesting place if you take the time to look around.

7. Rules keep kids safe, and health and safety are a parent's top responsibilities.

8. Impoliteness is not okay. No name-calling, teasing, bullying, kicking, or hitting.

9. If you don't take care of yourself, you'll get tired, cranky and unhappy. If you go days without taking care of yourself you'll exhaust your family as well.

10. Never, ever withhold love.

WEEK 24
The Family Business

Family Harmony is the business of your family. Parents are the CEOs but the kids need to know your goals for the family, your philosophy, your expectations, and your "business" plan.

Having a plan (and parents following through on the plan) takes the guesswork out of living in your home. It allows kids to feel secure and anchored. Accountability motivates, inspires, and creates problem-solvers. ("Hmmmm, what will happen if I paint an elephant on my bedroom wall? Ah yes! I get to clean it up!)

Successful businesses chart their expectations, their follow-through and their progress. This creates a work culture where everyone is on board. So too with families.

Make sure that your family expectations (rules) are posted, as well as what's not acceptable and how that will be handled by the CEO.

Rules are not about control. Rules are about clearly conveying your family's culture and philosophy of harmony. Your kids will make bad choices at times. You can't control that, but you can let them know "Here are the consequences of poor choices, and here are the rewards of good choices."

Consistency is ***King!*** When adults live their message, there is mutual respect. No one is confused, frustrated or angry.

There are numerous examples of companies that failed their employees. They made decisions contrary to the expectations they set forth. They thought about their gain and not the workers well-being. They turned their companies into fearful, petty places.

Don't let your "business" become a secondary consideration.

WEEK 25
Rules for Parents by Ben & Malka

Ben is 8, Malka is 5 and they are the best of friends. They want to tell you the rules and consequences that they made up for parents!

Ben and Malka think that parents need rules, too. I agree. Ben and Malka think that parents shouldn't be allowed to misbehave. I agree. Ben and Malka think that if parents got punished for misbehavior, they would be nicer to their children. I think I agree; at least I agree mostly. (I'm not real fond of the word "punishment.")

Rules for parents by Ben and Malka:

1. No yelling
2. No taking away dessert as a punishment

3. Don't spank the dog
4. Play more games with us
5. Help me with my homework and don't get mad if I don't understand
6. Sit with me until I fall asleep
7. I like to talk to Mommy when I'm taking a bath
8. I want chocolate-chip pancakes on Saturdays
9. We know how to dress ourselves
10. Don't say mean things

Here is what parents get if they break those rules:

1. No dessert for you
2. No TV for 2 days
3. Take us to the zoo
4. Buy us pizza
5. You clean our rooms

I see our future President and Secretary of State, but I'm not saying which one is which!

WEEK 26
Some People Just Don't Get It

What is the one thing about motherhood that makes you feel misunderstood?

Becoming a mother changed everything. I've heard from scientists that there are actual chemical changes that occur in the mother shortly after birth that help with attachment, which of course is key to a child's survival. I'm not sure if the changes are permanent, but in my experience they were. It was as if one day I was my old self and then... poof! I gave birth and became someone else, someone's mother. And I haven't been my old self since, and it's been 26 years!

So what is the thing people don't "get"? It's that overwhelming, all encompassing, deep biological love and yearning to be near my kids.

I still think my kids are the most interesting, adorable, smart, funny, amazing people I've ever met. I long to talk to them, I can't wait to be with them and I miss the ability to just reach out and touch them every chance I get.

Don't get me wrong, I do not stalk my kids, I don't call them everyday and I restrain myself from too much PDA. I do like my space. I like the quiet. I like not being a slave to their schedules. My husband and I enjoy our alone time, too.

But it's hard!!!!! The early experience of being with them all the time is like a template in my psyche.

Once upon a time, it was sleepless nights, endless diaper changes, nursing, weaning, comforting. Today it's long distance calls, cross country visits, emails and texts. But the longing is still there, in the air, over the cables, through the Internet. And sometimes, when the timing is just right, it's in a nice long hug.

WEEK 27
No Such Thing as Lazy

Go-getter
Noun, informal
An aggressively enterprising person.

I live in Seattle. It is a city of Go-Getters. We're the home to Google, Starbucks, Amazon, Mike's Hard Lemonade, and Nordstrom. Pretty much everything started in Seattle.

Then you have your "Go-Getter Parents." Go-Getter Parents believe that if you're not moving forward, at a gallop, you're just lazy and you'll amount to nothing. Go-Getter Parents are worriers and that's a tough way to be parented. Perhaps some of you are familiar with this style from your own years as a kiddo with a Go-Getter Parent?

So what do you do when you have a child whose energy level doesn't match your own, and you feel like you're dragging them through life?

1. Take some time to observe your child's style. Some of us are just faster and more decisive than others. Some of us are more deliberate. We need to weigh the merit/loss potential of every situation. This isn't something you can change – it's just the way people are, no matter how much you push or bribe them.

2. Sometimes, what looks like procrastination is really burn-out. Ask questions. Be gentle. Burn-out or exhaustion isn't simply an attitude. It can signal a medical challenge – physical, emotional, or both.

3. Assume the best about your child. Perhaps your child needs more of your time to complete certain tasks, perhaps they need more guidance. That's okay. We're not all good at everything, even if we live in Seattle!

I don't believe in "Lazy." It's **always** something else. When people are given the physical and emotional support to release fear and recharge, they can re-engage with more focus and dedication.

WEEK 28
Soul Music

My son began playing piano at the age of four and a half, barely old enough to read, his little feet not even grazing the floor under the bench. He gravitated toward the piano like some kids are drawn to a basketball court or a football field. Before school, when he was ready early, instead of playing on the computer or watching TV he'd sit down and practice. My own memories of piano lessons involve threats and bribes so I was unprepared for this completely natural love affair my son has with the piano.

"But really," people ask, "how did you do it?" Here's the secret… I love my son and it makes me immeasurably happy when he's happy. So, I encouraged him. I listened to his practicing for hours, sometimes so loudly I couldn't talk on the phone. I drove him to lessons. I asked questions. I listened to the music he was playing, as well as the music in his soul, and I made it important to me, personally, to participate in his passion.

These days it's so easy to fall prey to the latest craze all the other kids are into. As parents we want our kids to keep up, to be marketable, to be competitive. But not every child's gifts are obvious early on and not every child finds his passion at age four. And sometimes, your child's interests may surprise you. But every human being deserves to be supported in his quest for meaning in this life, and as parents it is our job to be their champion.

I don't know where my son's journey will take him. At 23, he doesn't know either. But I do know this: whatever is important to him is important to me.

We all have some music in our souls and, as a mom, I just want to listen to my children's soundtracks.

WEEK 29
"I've Been Accepted!"

Love feels great. Everybody gets their own personal high from loving and being loved.

Acceptance, on the other hand, can be painful, especially when it comes to family. We think that if we accept the status quo, our kids won't ever dream or expand their horizons. For parents, that is a scary thought. Who wants to think of helping their 40-year-old with his laundry? Or driving her to the doctor? Or waking him up to get to work on time?

We fear that acceptance will lead our kids to a life of dependence, lazy thinking, and no motivation. In fact, a parent's acceptance gives kids the foundation to try new things, to be courageous and adventurous. It promotes independence, creativity, and critical thinking.

Acceptance often gets mixed up with approval, but they're not the same at all. Approval implies agreement. Approval keeps us tied to praise from others and makes us less likely to make our own choices and less likely to honor our integrity.

Acceptance, on the other hand, means "I respect your ability to make choices and I respect your preferences."

When we push our own agenda, we let our kids know that they are not reliable, not responsible, not resourceful, and not smart. But when we keep our negative judgments to ourselves, we allow people to consider answers and solutions that may otherwise have been hidden.

When we deny our loved ones that sense of acceptance, we deny ourselves opportunities to laugh and hug and talk and share love. The question is, *"Do you want to love your family from afar or from up close?"*

WEEK 30
Good Cop, Bad Cop

I may be dating myself, but I remember watching shows like Adam 12 and Dragnet when I was a kid and being really curious about the dynamic between the officers. Usually one was warmer, and the other was pretty hard-boiled. The idea was for the good cop to gain the criminal's trust and then the bad cop to swoop in and try to break him down.

It occurred to me that some parents might use this "good cop, bad cop" tactic in dealing with discipline. It seems tempting because from a psychological perspective it makes sense. One parent can take the reasonable, non-punitive approach to elicit an admission of guilt or to coerce one child into tattling on another. The other parent can then mete out the punishment.

But this game can only lead to some major trust issues, especially once the child wises up and catches on, and in all likelihood she will. Not only will she not trust you, but she'll also get really messed-up ideas of marriage and her own impending motherhood. Ideas such as: parents play games, they're not straight with you, they don't respect each other to the extent that they're willing to burden each other, AND when I'm a parent, I'll have to trick my kids into behaving. This is a horrible lose-lose-lose-lose-lose situation.

So while it's sometimes tempting to use this "good cop, bad cop" technique I urge parents to resist. Creating an atmosphere of unity and trust between parents and between parents and child, strengthens the present and the future.

For this week, focus on building trust, creating a unified partnership between you and your spouse and between you and your children. And most of all, work to make your home one where peaceful communication and love can grow.

WEEK 31
Code Blue

There are times in our lives when we hit the wall, we have a crisis, or it's clear that *one thing* needs our attention now and for a while. That's when it's time for "Intensive Care."

In an intensive care scenario, everyone hones in on one issue. For example: Your child has just been diagnosed with ADHD *and* is falling behind in his/her school work. Rather than worrying about grades or popularity or whether she can organize her binder or remember to take out the trash, parents would do well to think about their child as being in the Intensive Care Unit. The ADHD is the major issue; not the grades.

"Go Small"

Instead of stressing out, "Go Small" for a bit - place some limitations on your life – do less, stay close, put away the less important things, lighten your schedule.

Parenting crises start in the heart and it's the heart that needs to be healed first. It may look like an attitude problem or a running away problem, or a defiance problem, but those are merely symptoms. When hearts are broken, that is precisely where to start – on the inside.

I was hired by a lovely family to work with them and their ADHD children. We were going to start that very evening when I got a call from the mother. They had just come from the doctor and had discovered that their daughter was burning herself on purpose.

What would you do?

We decided to postpone ADHD coaching until the self-mutilation was under control. Deal with the heart first. Executive skills can wait. The first order of business is to keep this child alive.

WEEK 32
Anger Journal

Even our "perfect" family had a secret.

The dirty little secret in my family is that my dad was a very angry guy. Not just temperamental, mind you. No, his was the raging, sarcastic, mean type of anger that could turn in a heartbeat from a horrible tantrum to a silence that would drag on for days. And the silence was the worst. It was scary and confusing never knowing when it would come, how long it would last, or what had caused it.

As an adult, I too have struggled with anger, but I've learned that most of the time it's a cover for other feelings. Whatever the reason, anger is scary for kids.

It's important to state that anger can also be a healthy emotion. When expressed properly, anger can foster greater understanding between people and it can bring clarity about one's feelings. But knowing your anger is the key; do you rage, curse, seethe or go silent?

As parents we model behavior for our kids and angry behavior is part of it. *But most of us don't give much thought to teaching about it.* I recommend keeping an "Anger Journal" to document your anger. Like any other journal, it's a great tool for understanding your own behavior. And an "Anger Journal" also sheds light on some potential triggers.

One final thing I must stress: anger should never be expressed with physical violence. Even in his darkest times, my dad never laid a hand on us. If you are ever tempted to strike your child, walk away from the situation and seek out professional help. Psychic wounds are painful and lasting, but there are some physical wounds from which there is no recovery.

WEEK 33
Got Garlic?

There are vampires all around us. Do you have your garlic?

You know I'm not talking about real vampires but about those people and activities that suck out our energy and make us feel foggy-brained and lethargic. What's tricky about vampires is their uncanny ability to sneak up behind, doing their dirty work before we have a chance to protest or run away. They're ...

1. The relatives who always complain.
2. The never-ending projects at school or work.
3. The concepts that bore us.
4. The day-in and day-out of everyday life.

5. Homework!

6. The ADHD children (or spouse) that demand attention just by their very existence. :-)

How do we protect ourselves from having the life sucked out of us? What can we do to reinvigorate our spirits when we find our energy has been sucked dry?

1. If you know which activities or people suck the life out of you, avoid them.

2. If you can't avoid them, limit your time with them or have a buddy by your side so you don't have to face the situation alone.

3. Or... find an alternative way to handle the situation (whether it's a task/activity or a person). Perhaps it's better to find a different location to engage.

4. "Bookend" it. Do something good for yourself before and after the event.

5. Journal about your anxiety before and after - what are you afraid will happen? What did happen and how did you feel?

6. Eat protein not carbs. Protein will give you energy to fight the good fight.

WEEK 34
Tweety Bird

Cruising the Twittosphere is hilarious. This week, we'd like to suggest that you compose your own Tweets (160 characters only). Really, it takes the edge off and can give you insights into what is truly going on in your house. And look! We left room for you to play! Some favorites of ours:

- HS #graduation. Where is my sweet 5 y.o? Time 2 contribute to his future therapy fund.

- I know eating ur own boogers helps immunity. What if ur gifted with someone else's? #Autism

- #NoteToSelf Sarcasm is lost on 2 year olds.

- I will never win an argument. Must. Surrender. Now. #ADHD #ADD

WEEK 35
Cell Phones Off!

Today as I was driving around town, a song came on that reminded me of my son and the mornings we would be alone in the car on the way to school. It was a sweet memory and I instantly called and left him a quick "I love you, have a great day" message.

The experience got me thinking about the time I spent in the car with all of my kids. For me it was golden time because we were all captive together, on the road to somewhere, with no interruptions.

Parents often use car time as a chance for them to impart some piece of "wisdom" to their captive audience. Then they wonder why the kid is texting or playing a game on their cell phone. Those parents are missing the point.

There is a payoff to all this driving and listening. I got to know my kids really well. I spent time with them when they were unguarded and receptive. I asked questions I could never ask at home and I got answers. It was a unique time that we shared together most days; time we all remember now. Those conversations are ones we revisit and reminisce about. When a familiar song comes on the radio now, it conjures up memories for all of us.

So the next time you're in the car with your kids, use your ears. Listen with them to their music (you can stand it, I promise!), listen to their conversation, ask questions. You are making memories, especially while sitting in traffic!

WEEK 36
Schools Are Not Battlegrounds

Teachers and parents are often adversaries, but that doesn't have to be the case. Schools are not battlegrounds and teachers aren't the enemy. Sure there are less than awesome school districts but you will always find teachers who will sympathize with you, and do whatever it takes to guide your child to excellence.

At the same time, there are parents who are unreasonable. It happens. There was the mom that told me her son was getting detention because I marked him tardy when he was late (tardy) to school. There was the father who was offended that I had a zero-tolerance policy for racial, sexual, and religious slurs.

In an effort to bring teachers and parents together, here are five things that teachers want you to know about supporting your children at school:

1. It is the student's job to impress the teacher, with work, with manners, with respect, with friendliness. Even one of those will suffice.

2. Two heads are better than one. Find another adult (or several adults) to help you parent your child. It really does take a village.

3. Children develop at different rates. It doesn't make them better or worse than each other. Mistakes are a normal part of development. Let them make mistakes.

4. Don't sit back and expect the school to teach everything your child needs to know. Encourage a love of all kinds of knowledge at home, on weekends, and during vacations.

5. Be the adult you'd like your child to become.

WEEK 37
Our Greatest Fear
In Memory of Sandy Hook, December 2012

Right now my babies are alive and well and have safely reached young adulthood. But 20 other precious little souls will never reach puberty, get a driver's license, vote, go to college and have the future their parents dreamed of.

For me, this tragedy brings my deepest fears out from the dark corners of my mind. The unimaginable that we parents shove far away from our consciousness, otherwise we might not be able to do our job: The job of raising children in a treacherous world. The job of helping them to feel safe enough to leave our nests and fly off.

My kids are fearless. They travel to far away places. They embrace adventure. You could say we did a good job of helping them to believe that the world is a wonderful and wondrous place. Of course they can't know the worry we have for their safety. They haven't yet experienced a parent's perspective on the dangers that seem to lurk everywhere.

I am like the parents of those young teachers, their careers barely begun, their whole futures unfolding. Finally, after all the sleepless nights, sacrifices and hard work you can breathe and enjoy the adults they have become. You look forward to the next phase in your parent/child adventure, becoming both a friend and a trusted advisor. But those plans have been destroyed, a reminder that we're never far from tragedy.

We parents live in a strange place. We walk the line between dreams and reality. The dreams that we have for our children's futures and the reality of the world that is. This past week, reality came crashing in with a vengeance. And it all happened in a place where dreams begin.

WEEK 38
Fearless Listening

Hearing is done with your ears. It's a physiological function. Listening is done with your ears, your mind, and your heart. It is physiological, mental, and emotional.

Your kids can deliver the same piece of information to you and, depending on whether you're hearing or listening, you can have an easy moment or a tense moment.

Real listening is fearless listening. Fear tells us to attack, judge, yell, deny, lecture, or interrupt. Fearless listening means hearing and accepting what's being shared. It requires vulnerability and that can be scary.

Fearless Listening is:

Attentive: You need to actually pay attention. You want to be careful not to interrupt, of course.

Non-judgmental: You don't have to agree with them, but don't judge them as being wrong or stupid or bad.

Non-correcting: Kids and parents can spend a lot of time trying to convince the other person of their point of view. It's not helpful and prolongs the misery of miscommunication. Don't correct them; just listen.

Loving, rather than defensive: Assume the best. If it sounds like an attack, assume it's fear speaking. You may feel the urge to run or to stay and fight, but try to stay and connect with your own heart.

Self-reflective: Conversations and heart-to-heart communications give you the chance to grow and learn more about yourself. Take these opportunities to ask yourself, "What's my part?" and "Can I be doing something differently, or have I been the best *me* I can be?"

WEEK 39
Brand-New Teenage Girl

Tweenage and teenage girls are a curious breed. They need and want help and, also, they *don't* want help. One moment they think you're the best parents in the world and the next, they hate you. May I offer some advice?

1. It's important for girls to know that they are in control of their bodies and their minds. Most teenage girls are insecure and rely on their friends to help them make decisions. *Give your tween/teen permission to say "no" when she feels uncomfortable in a situation.*

2. Learn how to walk the line between *just listening vs. offering advice*. Girls can get defensive very quickly, so asking "curious

questions" works best. Start with "I'm curious why you feel that way…" or "I'm curious to know your thinking on this…" It keeps the emotion out of the situation and helps them really focus their thoughts.

3. *Don't judge.* This applies to everything from their friends and boyfriends to lying, gossiping, or bullying. If your teen asks you about your own past, share what you're comfortable with *and the lesson you learned from the situation.* Often they simply want reassurance that they're on the right track. So a simple "why do you ask?" can help you avoid telling too much.

4. *Ask your teen if they want you to intervene before you just do it.* Sometimes teens want you to make a phone call or set up a meeting, but if you don't ask first, you run the risk that they won't trust you with their feelings next time. (Note: for emotionally or physically dangerous situations, intervene ASAP).

You are the navigator but not the captain. Chart a course, share ideas, listen, ask questions, don't judge and let them know you are there.

WEEK 40
Happiness. Sigh.

Whether you believe that a Higher Power makes the decisions, or that things happen randomly, it's super important to have a good attitude. *Or at least to pretend that you do. Yes, pretending works just as well.*

I am no Pollyanna. Truthfully, I wish people would get their acts together so that I could be happy. It's just not how it works. I've learned that negative, "Bah! Humbug! Thinking" is pretending that bad things are true, *so why not pretend good things instead?*

1. **Smile away your resentments**. Put on a big crazy grin and start talking to yourself. It's probably not a great idea to do this publicly unless you're okay with

people thinking you're off your rocker. However, this technique does work. You'll be surprised how quickly you get happy.

2. **Say "Thank You" for every situation.** This is a big bummer. It's so much easier to wallow in self-pity. Only thing is, it doesn't do anything to lift our spirits and, as parents, we need a whole lot of Spirit-Lifting. "Thank you for this experience" is hard to say but super powerfully positive.

3. **You can only change yourself.** Big freaking bummer, I know. It *feels* like your spouse or your child or your job or the school system is the source of your unhappiness, but they're not. It's all about your insides and how you *want* to feel. You may not be confident, but do you *want* to be? That's the $100,000 question!

Look, here's the deal: I've tried it every other which way. If there were another way, I would have found it for sure. I'm actually doing you a favor; I'm saving you time and energy.

You're welcome.

WEEK 41
The Last One is Dessert

Many of my friends thought I was a little crazy to have a third child since we already had a healthy girl and boy. But my husband and I both believed there was one more waiting to join our family. In fact when he was born and I first laid eyes on him I just thought, "Oh, there you are! I've been waiting for you!" He was immediately so familiar to me I felt as if he was always a part of our family.

When I was expecting, I had a wonderful doctor with a great sense of humor. She said the third child is like the dessert - that perfect, sweet finish to a great meal. It was such a lovely sentiment and one that I have remembered these last 20 years.

Parenting this last child has been so exciting and fun and bittersweet. Every milestone with him has been new and unique, but it has also been the last time I'll nurse a baby, the last time I'll see a little one off to kindergarten, the last of the new drivers, the last prom and graduation. The last teenager!

Time goes by so fast. Before you know it, you're an empty-nester. But it's possible to making lasting memories for your family – You can create a Family Bucket List. Create it together!

Do it now, at the beginning. Your lives are unfolding in amazing and fantastic ways. Make sure you take the time to breathe, to reflect, to be grateful, to make lasting memories, and to love.

Brian is the dessert in our family, but this family's journey is just picking up steam. We're not done, by any stretch of the imagination! To all of my children, now adults: thanks for the ride of a lifetime! We made it! Now, let's see what comes next!

WEEK 42
Choosing Step-Motherhood

When I was young, I assumed I would have children of my own. I was born in the late 50's and this is what women did. We had children. And then, a funny thing happened to me on the way to motherhood... I chose step-motherhood instead.

This was (and still is) absolutely one of the right-est decisions I've ever made. Here is the nutshell version of the years-long, angst-ridden analysis I went through that led to my revelation: *I was not built to be a mom; I was built to be a step-mom.*

They say "It takes a village to raise a child" and on some very important level, I love the idea of being part of a larger body of family members. Large-larger, not just 5 or 6 people larger. I'm a better me when I can share the responsibilities, sort of wend my way through the crowd, interacting with a variety of people when I'm needed (or want to) and having alone time when I'm not needed.

Step-parenting is the village I've longed for. We are a group dedicated to encouraging and loving two young people. I love being an additional parent. I love being able to enjoy my step-kids growing and finding joy for themselves. And I love supporting them – using my strengths to build theirs.

Choosing step-parenting was the right decision for me, and now I am a grandmother (we've dropped the "Step") and even though I adore my precious granddaughter, and thoroughly enjoy spending hours of time with her, I'm happy that she is blessed with a *village* of people who care for her and love her unconditionally.

WEEK 43
Create Your Own Family Holidays!

Break the rules! It's not like you're hurting anyone. It's not like your decision will alter the course of the universe. But it could alter your family relationships: you could grow closer, you could enjoy each other more, you could laugh more, and you could relax more.

September 2 is my birthday but it's not *just* my birthday. Apparently it's also "National Beheading Day." No lie; look it up. There's even a process if you want to make your holiday official.

Have fun. Go Random. Have a family contest. Include your *whole* family, not just your immediate family:

- **Funny Dress-Up Day** - the winner chooses what's for dinner or dessert.

- **Hug-before-Speaking Day** - Before you speak you have to hug the person you're about to talk to. (This sounds like a holiday Barbara's mother would create!)
- **Don't Bug Dad/Mom Day** - Right? On Don't Bug Dad Day, all requests and complaints go through Mom. On Don't Bug Mom Day, they go through Dad.
- **No Words Day** - everything has to be communicated through gestures or pictures.
- **Appreciate Someone Day** - everybody chooses 1-3 people that they appreciate and then they write them a note.
- **Dessert Instead of Dinner Day**
- **Wash the Dog Day** (driest person gets out of chores for a week)
- **Talent Show Day**
- **Happy Vegetable Day** – all meals are made with vegetables (veggie omelet, veggie burgers, zucchini or carrot bread, spinach/raspberry ice cream.

Really, the sky's the limit. Just have fun!

WEEK 44
Love Means Having to Say "I'm Sorry"

When we are raising our kids, we want them to look up to us, to respect us and to believe that we are capable of guiding them through childhood.

It's tempting to believe that we are always right, that we have all the answers. For those of us who might have felt unheard during our own childhood, being a parent can overwhelm us with the feeling that finally, we can demand to be listened to and obeyed.

"Good-enough parents don't lecture, yell, nag or act smug ... much."

This is Principle #2 in the *Good-Enough Parenting Manifesto*. What we're really saying is that Good-Enough Parents act with kindness, compassion and respect toward their children. And that includes admitting a mistake and apologizing.

It is not a sign of weakness or a capitulation to your kids to say you're sorry. It's human! And don't we all want our kids to learn how to be human? It's also a great lesson to teach our kids that not having all the answers is not a failure.

Apologizing to someone is never easy. These days, people do it via email, text or on Facebook. And while something is better than nothing, I believe a face-to-face *mea culpa* is the most respectful and effective way to admit a mistake and ask for forgiveness.

Loving someone means feeling safe enough to be vulnerable, to allow yourself to feel that unconditional love coming back to you when you say "I'm sorry. Please forgive me."

It also means being humbled by that unconditional love and being willing to accept that we do hurt each other at times, even by accident.

WEEK 45
Gift-Giving That Doesn't Stink

I make a big deal about spoiling kids. I was a spoiled kid and it didn't do me any good. Not even a teensy-weensy bit. *After all, it's called "Spoiled" because it stinks.*

These are my top three gift-giving MUSTS:

1. Limit the number of gifts you give. *More* (in general) is confusing for children, and *more gifts* is practically a recipe for future disappointment. They will confuse love, self-worth, friendship, happiness, and well-being with the amount or cost of the gifts they get and give.

2. Set a gift budget with the members of your family and stick to it, even if it's hard. This teaches children about limits

and about respecting one's own and another's boundaries. It also teaches about mutual trust as boundaries which are broken, even for something as great as a cool present, subtly teaches that that person's word cannot be trusted.

3. Saying "Thank you" and sending thank-you notes are a lost art. Whether you call it Gratitude, Follow-up, or Politeness, the foundation of good relationships and good business practices is a well-thought out and well-composed "Thank You."

Giving and receiving gifts can teach kids about generosity, gratitude, appreciation, selflessness, saving, budgeting, and investing money.

Teach your children good manners and help them become more social and successful beings.

And remember, it's always a "best practice" for parents to set an example for their children in all these areas.

WEEK 46
My Favorite Mood & Energy Boosts

Gratitude Lists - every day write down at least ten things that you're grateful for. You don't have to limit yourself to big things like being grateful for your health or your family - though those are good choices! Sometimes I write that I'm grateful for sweatpants or tacos or my smartphone! Be on the lookout for as many interesting events, happy coincidences, fun encounters or even close calls that surprise you.

Affirmations - We give ourselves so many negative messages and think they're the truth, so it's important to counter them with equally powerful, positive statements. You can find affirmations in books or you can create your own. One way to write an affirmation is to take a negative statement and turn it around. "I am ugly" becomes "I am beautiful." Another technique is to take one of your less charming attributes and state the opposite. "I am judgmental," becomes "I accept my children just the way they are." Yet another technique is to create a statement that reflects your deepest dreams *in present tense.* For example, "I am an emotionally-available parent."

Prayer and meditation - Prayer is often underestimated. If you feel comfortable with it or if you'd *like* to feel comfortable with it, just start a conversation with God/the Universe/Higher Power. I find that I get the best results when I'm not making self-centered or materialistic requests. Praying for peace of mind is a good one.

You can't *worry* your way to solving a problem and you can't *worry* your way to better health or more happiness. Instead, try these techniques and teach them to your children as well!

WEEK 47
Don't Take Things Personally

"Good-enough parents work really, really, really hard to not take things personally."

Think of your tweens and teens as toddler-adults, ready to take off but without sufficient life skills. They are encountering adult emotions, expectations, dreams, body changes, triumphs and disappointments. *Yet they are still kids in many ways.*

Remember when they were toddlers and they would throw tantrums for lack of a better way to express their needs and their frustrations?

Tweens and teens also throw tantrums in the face of challenges that they have no clue how to handle. The sulking, the "eye-daggers," the shouting, the slamming doors, and the isolation are all versions of a Teen Tantrum and *you do not need to take it personally*. These episodes indicate that your toddler-adults are up against something that they do not understand. Whether your children ask for help or not, help is what they would like.

It's really important for you to be as calm as possible. For example, if your children were in extreme physical pain and didn't want you to touch them, you wouldn't take it personally. You would try to be as calm as possible and also as reassuring as possible.

But when our kids are in emotional pain and say hateful things or yell a lot, we take it personally and we fire back at them with similar ammunition. It doesn't work, does it?

The trick is to be calm. Parenting takes time. Lose your own agenda and listen to what your child is trying to tell you. Ask questions - not the interrogating kind but things like, "How can I help?" or "What's a fair solution for all of us?"

Changing habits takes time but it is worth it, and so is your family!

WEEK 48
Do We Ever Live Up To Our Potential?

I was sitting around the other day, wondering: "Do we ever live up to our potential? And if so, when does it happen? And if not, is that okay?"

Teachers and parents make judgments about a child's potential based on intelligence or talent — we're smart, we're musical, we're athletic, and so on. But this determination neglects to take into account the whole person, and I think that's a huge problem.

What if our emotional maturity or emotional fluency is what determines whether we live up to our potential? Or what if it's determined by our mental health rather than by our intellectual possibilities?

I think we make choices about our future, even our immediate futures, based on an emotional tug. For some that emotional tug is pleasing our parents, for some it's pleasing our friends, for others it's pleasing ourselves. Still others have a sense of duty to God, country, or some other group. And, more and more, we see kids creating their own definition of potential.

Then, too, who said potential was something to be measured in childhood? *Maybe we shouldn't have that conversation until our kids our 30 or 40. Then we can say, "Wow! You've lived up to your potential!"*

Before I was 40, I still hadn't reached the potential I've reached in the last 15 years. I don't think Potential is stagnant; I think it's something that changes and expands as we change and expand.

There aren't just ten careers out there; there are thousands. Why pigeonhole and even, limit, our kids by declaring so early that they're not living up to their potential? Perhaps at ten years old we should focus more on their humanity, hmmm?

WEEK 49
Divorce Do's & Don'ts

You're getting divorced. Your kids are shaken and you are a jumble of emotions. And now you have to craft a parenting plan. No small feat, to be sure. Here are DO's and DON'Ts to guide your decisions:

-- DO be consistent. This isn't about you and your ex. This is about your kids. Forget convenience. Divorce isn't convenient. If you want your kids to thrive despite this upheaval, *you need to be willing to be uncomfortable for their sake.*

-- DO keep a consistent *weekly* schedule

-- DO keep a consistent *daily* schedule.

-- DON'T bring new people into your time together or into your home until you are in a committed long-term relationship. If you end the relationship, you're not the only one to suffer *and your kids learn that relationships are fleeting and people are heartbreakers.*

-- DO be an adult. Your child is not your confidant and is not responsible for your emotional, physical, spiritual, or financial well-being.

-- DO be responsible for upholding your behavioral expectations and consequences.

-- DO get help if you need it. If your car broke down, you wouldn't leave it on the side of the road and forget about it. Ignoring a problem won't repair your family either.

-- DO be light and polite always. No name-calling, taunting, teasing, or put-downs

-- DO Say "please" "thank you" "you're welcome" "excuse me"

-- DO listen when someone is speaking to you.

-- DON'T yell, nag, or lecture. Don't use an insulting or disrespectful tone of voice when speaking to each other.

WEEK 50
Obedience Training

Let me tell you about our dog, Akiva. He was 45 pounds of undying devotion, and SPIRIT. He liked to sit in wet dirt, jump into my face, and pee on every. single. bush and tree. And he was all ours.

Our goal was for him to stop being so hyper-animated, but we didn't take actions to meet that goal. We didn't take him (and ourselves) for training.

He was just so cute and cuddly, and we thought he'd grow out of it eventually. He didn't. He grew more insistent and more attached to being the idiosyncratic pup that he always was.

Training would have provided us with

consistent responses to his cuckoo behaviors. That would have saved us from the broken screen at our friends' house ($50), the book he ate one Christmas ($17.95), and the long wall of torn curtains in our living room ($100s) And still we said, "He can't help it. He's our ADHD dog. He's co-dependent. He has separation anxiety. It's not his fault."

In short, *we had a goal but we didn't want to do the work to achieve it. We excused his behavior and made excuses for him.*

So what's your goal for your kids? Not what job you'd like them to have but what kind of person would you like them to be? Courteous, Generous, Emotionally healthy? Bold, Outrageous, Independent?

List your goals and then plan your parenting around actions, behaviors, and attitudes that will encourage positive growth in those areas. Then, as in dog training, be consistent.

And if it's not working, don't make excuses, get help! It'll save you money and grief in the long run.

WEEK 51
If Kids Wrote Your New Year's Resolutions

I hear a lot from kiddos and they pretty much all tell me the same things, regarding what they would change about their parents:

1. **Stop Yelling**. For kids, nagging is the same as yelling. Your voice may not be raised but if you're nagging them, they call it yelling. We yell over ridiculous stuff and we yell because *they're* yelling. More "don'ts" that fit here: teasing, imitating, lecturing, acting smug and being sarcastic. Let's be bigger than that.

2. **Don't make such a big deal about grades**. Kids - especially as they get older - know how important grades are. It

would be hard NOT to know. Grades are proclaimed as their ticket to success. That's not totally true though, and the pressure kids feel to perform is creating **tidal waves of anxiety in the younger generation**. Don't let your fear or your pride get in the way of your kids' mental health.

3. **Spend more time with them**. Even the surliest teen wants to spend more time with you! One of my clients didn't like that her dad stayed up til 3 am playing computer games because then his whole schedule was different than the rest of the family. Another wanted her mother to stop swearing. One boy asked his mother to stop frowning so much. Another boy asked his dad to eat cereal with him at night.

If you ask your kids, it's really interesting what they'll say.

WEEK 52
Thanks To Our Teachers

When we were young we watched TV and learned how to become decent kids. Our mentors were Sheriff John, Engineer Bill, Captain Kangaroo, and Mr. Rogers

We learned:

- Eat healthy food, like carrots and milk.
- Celebrate people's birthdays.
- Try new things.
- Make friends of all sorts.
- Ask questions - your mind is a garden.
- Make a wish. Make a lot of wishes!

ABOUT THE AUTHORS

Margit Crane

Step-mom, grandma, and Family Coach, Margit Crane is passionately devoted to making growing up much easier for ADD/ADHD kids, discombobulated tweens & teens, and the stressed-out parents who love them! A 35-year veteran teacher and school counselor, Margit is the Moms Choice Award®-winning author of the family-friendly, delightfully funny ***How to Train Your Parents in 6 1/2 Days*** available on Amazon.com.   Contact her at MargitCrane.com

Barbara Dab

Mom to three grown kids and journalist, Barbara also works with small business owners to help raise public awareness with an eye toward growth. Barbara Dab believes in the power of communication. In both her personal and professional lives she strives to connect with those around her through positive interactions. Barbara is a former news reporter from Los Angeles where she covered the hard stuff, and now hosts a public affairs show in Nashville, TN.

Check out Good-Enough Parenting on Facebook and Twitter.

Listen to "Good-Enough Parenting" on Chat with Women radio.

Get some family support - GEParentingInfo@gmail.com

Made in the USA
Middletown, DE
19 January 2016